And Baby Makes Zero

Teresa Acre

ISBN:1530560268
ISBN-13:978-1530560264

Forward

Finding out you are pregnant should be a wonderful thing. Thinking about all the changes that will be taking place in your life. Anticipating all the new emotions you will feel, especially when your baby is placed in your arms for the first time. The absolute wonder you will have when you look this precious little person in the eyes, knowing that you had a part in creating life. That moment when you know your life has been altered forever, and that it is definitely a good thing.

This book "And Baby Makes Zero" explains what happens when the decision is made to abort a baby. What should be a happy time in a person's life becomes a traumatic experience that leaves women AND men wounded and changed, even if they don't know it at the time. When abortion is chosen the baby is gone, many times the relationship ends, and both mother and father are changed forever.

I could spend many words on these pages sharing statistics and research about what happens when a child is aborted, but I prefer to just tell my story.

May you be blessed as you read.

CONTENTS

Dear Reader –

I have written this book to share the honest truth about the sadness of having an abortion, and how it negatively affects a person. This book is not intended to bring shame, guilt, or hurt. The purpose of this book is to be honest, because the truth is that there is hope, forgiveness, encouragement, and healing after abortion. This is my personal story about my experience having gone through abortion. It is also my journey of forgiveness and healing. I believe this book has passion with a purpose.

Please read gently but truthfully.

John 8:32 ...*and you will know the truth, and the truth will set you free.*

ACKNOWLEDGMENTS

A huge thank you to all who have made this possible.
Thank you to my beautiful daughters, Brandy and Megan,
for the cover photo. Thank you to my son-in-law Josh for
editing and patience. Most importantly thank you to God,
because this was His idea.

Scripture quotations are from:

The Holy Bible, English Standard Version (ESV).
Copyright © 2001 by Crossway, a publishing ministry of
Good News Publishers.

1

THE BEGINNING OF UNDERSTANDING

Somewhere between my 20's and turning 50 I grew to dislike the seasons of fall and spring. It is one of those feelings that crept up on me and became a part of who I was. For no apparent reason, I began to call the seasons of fall and spring the "in-betweens." I felt that summer and winter were the desired seasons, while fall and spring were meant to just be endured. The fact is, living in Michigan the seasons of fall and spring can be neurotic and messy. I assumed that was the reason for my dislike of them.

It was only somewhere in my late 40's that I realized that fall and spring were the seasons that I had my abortions. The first was in the fall while I was in high school; the other was in the spring while I was in college. It was the abortions, not the weather that explained my dislike of the two seasons.

It had been decades since I had aborted two babies and still there was a subtle sadness about me. I could not seem to find true happiness. I had an underlying feeling that something was missing, or not right. I felt as if I had to always be reaching for the next thing, or constantly perfecting everything around me, including myself. I could never put my finger on it, or articulate it, it was just there. I now know that I was beginning to understand that going through abortion had changed me. I would soon learn more than I could have ever imagined about how much, and in what ways, abortion had changed me.

Ecclesiastes 3: *For everything there is a season, a time for every matter under heaven*

2

GROWING UP

Around the age of 30 God began to draw me to Him. I knew a little about God growing up, but not much. I was born in the city, but grew up on a farm. My father wanted us to have the farm experience so he moved us from the city when I was nine years old. We were a typical farm family. I was blessed to have both of my parents together, raising my siblings and myself. My father was employed away from home while my mother worked at home caring for all of us. It was a busy lifestyle and we worked hard as a family.

One sadness for me was that we never went to church as a family. I always desired for us to go together. I knew classmates went to church with their families. I would hear them talk about youth activities, and I even attended church services when I spent the night at my friend's house. But at home we did not go to church as a family. I was allowed to attend Sunday school periodically and the annual summer Vacation Bible School programs at our country church. The godly men and women at the church were so sweet. They loved on me and accepted me, and I will always be grateful for them. They made me feel important and that God loved me. They may never know what an impact they had on me. I am sure they prayed for me.

Some people say that it doesn't matter if you are raised in a Christian home, and that it has nothing to do with making the decision to abort a baby. I disagree. I believe that if I had been raised with godly values and challenged to stay sexually abstinent, I may not have made the choices I did.

Philippians 4:1...*stand firm thus in the Lord, my beloved*

3

LIFE AND THEN THE SURPRISE

Even though I was not raised in a Christian home, somehow God made Himself very real to me. By April of 1992, while eight months pregnant with my second child, something amazing happened. I had a true born again experience with Jesus. I had always known that something was missing from my life that college, career, marriage and even my own child could not fill. And now, for the first time in my life, I found what was missing. I told God that I would do whatever it took to feel whole and at peace. Up until this point in my life, and even though I didn't truly understand it at the time, I struggled with fear. I suffered silently with nightmares, and the dread of death, especially children. I remember one time while watching a football game on TV, I heard a baby crying in the crowd. I searched the TV screen intently, but did not even see a baby. It was so upsetting to me, and yet no one else could hear the baby. Looking back I realize my abortion experiences added to my fear, especially with children. To this day my husband honors me by watching sporting events on TV with the volume low or on mute.

I made the decision to change my life to live for God. A peace came over me that I had never felt before. Immediately things began to change. One of the most pronounced changes I noticed was my stand on the issue of abortion. I had previously wavered in my view on abortion. On one hand I didn't want anyone to experience what I had gone through. I had one child and was expecting my second child and was obviously supportive of life. On the other hand I had gone through abortion. How could I stand against it?

One of the first thoughts I had after saying yes to Christ was "abortion is wrong," period! It cannot be negotiated with God. It represents death. Just because it is legal does not mean it is moral. God is against abortion, because He represents life. I could no longer waver back and forth with my view of abortion. I decided to stand against it, regardless of what anyone said.

As I began to follow Christ things continued to change. It is so true that when you really get to know God, and His ways, your life changes. It's not like you wake up one morning and go through the day saying "I'm going to change this and I'm going to change that," it just happens. Learning how to love God and learning how He does things just changes you.

I passionately embraced motherhood, even leaving the business world to raise my children. I could not endure one more time where the babysitter knew two days before I did that my child had a new tooth. I wanted to raise my own children. I had this urge to be there for them. Research has shown that parents who are post abortive either 1) over connect with their earthly children or 2) under connect with their earthly children. For whatever reason we either throw ourselves into being super mom (or dad), or we feel a true "disconnect" with our earthly child(ren).

I was an "over connector!" I had this burning desire to be the best mom ever. I monitored everything in regards to my kids. Maybe you can relate. Studies of post-abortive people show that they sometimes try to atone for the aborted baby, or overly protect their earthly children because they did not protect the aborted child. This explains why I was always trying to be one step ahead, anticipating what would be needed or anticipating danger, etc. My kids didn't have to be great, but I had to be a great mother to them.

At this time in my life, as a new believer in Jesus Christ, I began to grow and learn more of God's ways not just the world's ways. I went on to have child number three who was a surprise package from God (we had only planned on two children). From the outside my life looked great. I graduated college, got a good job, married a classmate from high school and had three awesome children. Each of my children is a miracle, because many women are not able to conceive after abortion - especially the second abortion.

I was passionate, upbeat, hardworking and committed to my family. As I look back now I realize that my intense personality and commitment to my family, especially my kids, was yet another "side effect" of having had an abortion. I did not realize my motivation to be supermom came from not protecting the children I had aborted. I was very protective of my earthly kids. I was always trying to "get it right." At that time in my life I rarely let myself think about my abortions. It was as if I had shut the door on that part of my past, locked it, and threw away the key.

When my youngest was four years old, our family moved to northern Michigan, and settled into a wonderful country church. I began helping with the youth and before I could blink God called me into ministry. In 2005 I had finished my studies and was licensed as a Reverend in the state of Michigan. I was an official youth pastor. I was moving along and life "seemed" fine.

One day, out of the blue, a friend in ministry recommended our local CareNet (now Life Resources of Northern Michigan) Post Abortive Bible Study. This friend did not even know I was post abortive. I decided to take the bible study, called Forgiven and Set Free, to be able to minister to others (or so I thought). Little did I know God was going to take me on a journey. I knew He had forgiven me. Now I was about to experience what it felt like for Him to set me free.

Jeremiah 29:11 *For I know the plans I have for you, declares the Lord, plans for welfare and not for evil, to give you a future and a hope.*

4

BABY NUMBER ONE - THE MISSING
GRANDCHILD

To be set free and move forward I had to first go back.
Not to agonize, but to be honest about what I had been
through. Everyone takes a different path to be healed.
Going back was my path to be healed.

My life before my first abortion was that of a typical
teenager. I was active in sports, leadership organizations,
band, and was an honor student. As I stated earlier I was
not raised in a Christian home. The views and beliefs in
our family were based upon family tradition and culture,
not on God's moral laws. So when abortion was legalized
in 1973 it seemed like it was ok. A worldview, not a
Christian view, led to the concept that it was okay to abort
a baby.

I can honestly say that I do not remember my parents
ever challenging me to stay abstinent until marriage. I
don't remember much guidance in the area of boyfriends,

intimacy, or sex. I was in high school when I experienced "love" for the first time (or so I thought). I gave myself sexually to a very nice boy and became pregnant. Believe it or not I didn't even know I was pregnant. It was my first time having sex, and it was messy and awkward. Not anything like in the movies. I wasn't even sure we actually had sex.

When I began getting sick in the morning my mom confronted me and asked me if I was pregnant. I had no idea if I was or not. My pregnancy was confirmed after a visit to our family doctor. There were no at home private pregnancy tests back then. I sometimes wonder how my parent's processed this time in our family's life, or how my siblings did for that matter. I remember how disappointed and upset my mom seemed and how distant my dad seemed. It was like there was a heaviness in the air. I could feel the strain between my parents. Years later I learned that abortion affects everyone around you, not just the mom and dad of the baby.

I may never know all the details of what happened at that time in my life, but I do know that my dad decided that I would have the abortion. My mom, who was raised in the church, even though not walking with Christ at the time, told me years later how devastated she was over my dad's decision. She was more devastated because she was the one who took me to the clinic to have the abortion. The baby would have been her first grandchild.

Ecclesiastes 11:5 *As you do not know the way the spirit comes to the bones in the womb of a woman with child, so you do not know the work of God who makes everything.*

5

GONE BUT NOT DONE

I do not remember the actual abortion, although I do remember a lot of pain. I felt shots in my private area, followed by a great amount of pulling. I threw up, I bled, I slept. I think maybe I was in shock. And even though I didn't know it at the time, I slipped into depression.

In the six to 12 months after the abortion my grades slipped in school, I tried to kill myself twice, and as odd at it may seem I became even more interested in guys (just one of the many "side effects" of abortion that no one tells you about). It's as if one tragedy opens the doors to negative choices and behavior. I don't really know how to explain it, it just happens.

At home we never really talked about the abortion. I was left alone to process this sadness, as was my family. Roe vs. Wade had been passed, making abortion legal several years before this point in my life. Every night, at least it seemed to me, the abortion debate was on the news. I would lay on the floor watching the TV agonizing and suffering shame because of my abortion. I remember that anytime I would lay on my stomach I thought I could feel the heartbeat of the baby, like I was being reminded and punished for what I had done. How could something "legal" make me feel so awful about myself? It was a very confusing time in my life. I never really talked to anyone about it, a few girlfriends maybe. By the time I graduated several of the girls in my high school had already had at least one abortion. It was like abortion had become the new birth control.

James 1:15 *Then desire when it has conceived gives birth to sin, and sin when it is fully grown brings forth death.*

6

OH HOW WE REPEAT OUR MISTAKES

Fast forward five years. I was in college and in a relationship that wasn't healthy; when I found out I was pregnant again. He and I were like oil and water, but by the time I realized it I was head over heels in love. I very much wanted to keep the baby. Even more than I wanted to keep the first baby. I didn't tell many people but I felt pressure from all different directions that my life would be ruined if I kept the baby. I was on my way to a promising future, assuming I finished college. A baby would ruin everything. Today, a woman would have many avenues of help, even to finish college, but back then not so much. This time my family did not know of my decision to abort.

I remember more details about this abortion compared to my first one. I especially remember setting in the waiting room feeling like the room was spinning. I was setting in a comfortable arm chair, talking to the counselor, gripping the arm rests. She kept asking me if I was ok and if I was absolutely sure I wanted to have an abortion. I have wondered if she was an angel. From talking to other women who have had abortions, they don't remember any counselor being so persistent to ensure that a woman really wanted an abortion.

I felt trapped. My boyfriend was setting next to me and I wanted so badly for him to jump up and say "No, we are not having an abortion. I will marry you and we will raise this child." But he said nothing. This is another side effect of abortion. Wanting someone to come and rescue you. In his defense I am sure he was as torn as I was. I will probably never know. I pray that he is healed from our abortion experience.

Within one hour baby number two was aborted from my body. One of the saddest memories I have from that day was just before we left the clinic, the doctor was "joking" about my healing process, saying that we could resume having sex as soon as we felt like it. I did not think it was funny. I wondered if the doctor was hoping I would get pregnant again so he would have a repeat customer. It still amazes me how casual our culture treats abortion.

Again my grades slipped, I secretly cried a lot, and I was definitely depressed. I went through the motions of life, but felt numb and preprogrammed. I had family, friends, school and work but nothing gave me any joy. I felt like I was barely surviving. It was like constantly treading water in the deep end of the pool while trying desperately to get to the edge. It was exhausting.

Matthew 2:18 *A voice was heard in Ramah, weeping and loud lamentation, Rachel weeping for her children; she refused to be comforted, because they are no more.*

7

FACING THE NUMBNESS

Somehow I moved on. Some days it seemed impossible to get out of bed and care about anything. Looking back I realize that I had so much to look forward to in the worlds eyes, and yet inside I had grief that was dying to get out. I felt alone in a mass of people, mindlessly moving, because that's what I was supposed to do. Some days I seriously considered quitting school and running far away where no one would know me, giving me a chance to start over. I really believe that God was by my side through this time in my life. Even though I didn't know Him personally, I believe He carried me. I don't have any other explanation as to how I survived and had a decent life, except God!

However, there was still "numbness" when it came to my abortions. Years later, I had a dear friend who had a miscarriage. I remember how devastated she felt. She wondered if she had done something to cause the miscarriage. She even questioned food she had eaten, agonizing over every detail of the 12 weeks she had been pregnant. It shocked me to realize that she felt more grief for her child than I did the children that I had aborted. It made me very sad. God was getting my attention so that I could open the door to my past and begin to think about my abortions. He was so gentle, putting people and information in my path. He gave me time to process my thoughts and my feelings.

Romans 8:28 *And we know that for those who love God all things work together for good, for those who are called according to his purpose.*

8

TELLING MY CHILDREN THE TRUTH

Most people avoid telling their earthly children about their abortion experience. I believe that each person needs to ask God for guidance making this decision. Even though it was unbelievably hard, I knew it was the right thing for me to tell my children. God had already asked me to tell my story publically, so I had to tell my kids and give them time to process. As we worked through the shock and hurt, we grew closer together. Here are their stories.

My son, who is the oldest, was in his early teen years when the Holy Spirit prompted me to tell him. He was preparing for heart surgery, and it seemed so unfair to tell him at that time. I wrestled in my mind with God and it took me halfway through a three hour road trip to finally tell him. He was shocked, devastated and disappointed. He could not believe that I had an abortion. As a follower of Christ and a youth pastor he heard me preach the truth from God's word - that life comes from God and that we are to protect it. It hurt him that I had an abortion in my past. He had me up on a pedestal and I came crashing down. He once asked me, "Then I am not the oldest, am I?" Wow did that hurt. It hurt me even more to realize what this meant to him and how he was trying to understand all of it.

Today he is 26, married to my beautiful daughter-in-law and they have given me two amazing granddaughters. It brings me to tears thinking about how forgiving God is. Even after aborting His babies He still allows me to have my own children and even grandchildren.

My oldest daughter was around 13 years old when we were driving down the road and she brought up the subject of abortion. She had a classmate considering abortion and she was very upset because she was a champion for life. She was so concerned that she even asked if our family could adopt the baby so the friend would not abort. For some reason she asked me straight out "Mom you didn't ever have an abortion, did you?" I told her "Yes I did."

My precious first born daughter was angry. Her question was "How could you?" It took time to process through the pain. Today she is 24 and married to my awesome son-in-law who bravely served for my freedom in Afghanistan. He is a Wounded Vet and I am extremely proud him. They plan to have children as soon as the Lord allows.

My youngest daughter was 10 years old when one average day she asked me "Mom, did you have an abortion?" I told her "Yes I did." We sat down and talked. I told her pretty much what I had told her brother and sister. She looked at me and said "Have you asked God to forgive you?" I said, "Yes I have." Her response was "Then you are forgiven and I forgive you too."

Today she is 19 years old, married to a wonderful man whom she has been friends with for a very long time, and is a passionate defender of life. They just moved home so we could start a business together. Their plans are to have children as well.

It was a relief and release telling my children my story. I know I hurt them. It took time for them to heal. But I also know they will have my experience to help others. It was gut wrenching and time consuming, but for me definitely worth it.

> James 5:16 *Therefore, confess your sins to one another and pray for one another, that you may be healed.*

9

MY CHILDREN IN HEAVEN

In 1993, my mother-in-law lost her nine month battle to lung cancer and went home to heaven to be with the Lord.   It was a tremendous loss and shock, as she was the first parent between my husband and I to die. We were blessed as a family to gather at her bedside when the time came for her life on earth to end. Even though we knew that she would be with Jesus, and she would be out of pain and happy, it was incredibly sad to let her go. It is so hard to describe how it feels to be with someone when they breathe their last breath. Life is celebrated at its beginning, not usually at its end.

We were standing in her room just after she passed, comforting each other, when I had something unusual happen. Standing at the foot of her bed looking at her, I saw above her headboard a precious glimpse of heaven. I saw my mother-in-law smiling and healthy, very much alive. It shocked me at first, but I stared intently with joy. As I looked closer I could see that she was holding hands with preschool age children. They were so happy to be with her, giggling and twirling around in a circle. I was so happy for her. My mother-in-law loved children. She worked hard away from home, which included travel, so she did not have much time for her grandchildren. But when they were around she loved on them and loved rocking the babies.

I kept this vision to myself as we moved through the motions of visitation, her funeral service, and her burial. The vision was so sweet. I can still see a little boy with blonde curly hair and a little girl with long black hair. They were so happy holding hands and dancing in their little circle.

Several weeks later I shared with a friend what I had seen in the hospital. She said (knowing that I am post abortive) "I think God showed you your children in heaven." In prayer God confirmed to me what my friend has spoken. God had allowed me to see my children in heaven. He also told me their names. The little boy is named Stephen and the little girl is named Nicole. Someday I will meet them, but for now I thank God that He allowed me to see my children and know that they are happy and healthy in heaven with Jesus and their Grandma!

Matthew 18:10 *See that you do not despise one of these little ones. For I tell you that in heaven their angels always see the face of my Father who is in heaven.*

10

TODAY

I currently serve as lead pastor of our church in rural northern Michigan. I suppose I am the "poster child" for forgiveness. Not only did God forgive me, give me children, and grandchildren, but He has also given me a congregation to shepherd on His behalf. I am blessed beyond words. I feel a peace inside where there used to be anxiety, fear, and anger. I know that I sinned against God by having an abortion. But even more I know that He has forgiven me and set me free from the agony of my past decisions. He is a wonderful Papa God who allows me to use my past to help people, while protecting me from reliving the trauma of my pain.

It has been my privilege to counsel many people, but especially those who are post abortive. When I share my story with them, it allows them to open up. For many it is the first time telling their story. Recently a friend of mine asked God to see their child in heaven. The reaction for this precious parent was wonderful. Even while this person allowed grief to have its place, there was also amazing joy and peace. Only God can do that.

As I look forward to what this book can do for the kingdom of God, I pray that thousands will be healed. Healed in minds, hearts, and bodies. Healed in relationships. Healed in a relationship with Abba Father God. Healed, whole, restored, renewed, and excited for life.

Galatians 5:22-23 *But the fruit of the Spirit is love, joy, peace, patience, kindness, goodness, faithfulness, gentleness, self-control*

11

MY PRAYER FOR YOU

If you are post abortive this is my prayer for you:

My Papa God in heaven - I thank you that this person was able to read this book and be touched in a positive way. My heart aches for the pain that abortion has caused this person. Please set them on a path of healing, grace, and passionate love. Give them the future You planned for them, and remind them that You are prepared to forgive and restore. Thank You. In Jesus name. Amen!

If you are reading this book because you know someone who is post abortive this is my prayer for you:

Father in heaven - You know all hearts and you know how to reach all hearts. I thank You, knowing that You will make a way for this person to connect and help a precious sister or brother who is hurting. Bless this person's steps and guide them by Your Holy Spirit, so that healing may come quickly and completely. Amen

If you are reading this because you want to love on those who suffer silently after having an abortion, this is my prayer for you:

Father God, bless the person reading this book who desires to be bold for You, because they are modeling your son Jesus Christ in their desire to be moved with compassion to help others. Thank you for their willingness to love unconditionally and have a heart for those hurting. Bring those men and women who need healing from abortion to this person as soon as possible. Remind them to pray daily for those who still need Jesus. Amen

Galatians 6:9 *And let us not grow weary of doing good, for in due season we will reap, if we do not give up.*

Love, Teresa

ABOUT THE AUTHOR

Teresa Acre is pastor of Fresh Start Church in Northern Michigan. She is also co-owner of Simple Living. She lives with her husband, 2 cats and 5 fish. She is gratefully surrounded by her children, their spouses, her grandchildren and her mom. She believes God is good.

Made in the USA
Middletown, DE
31 January 2020